MW00941724

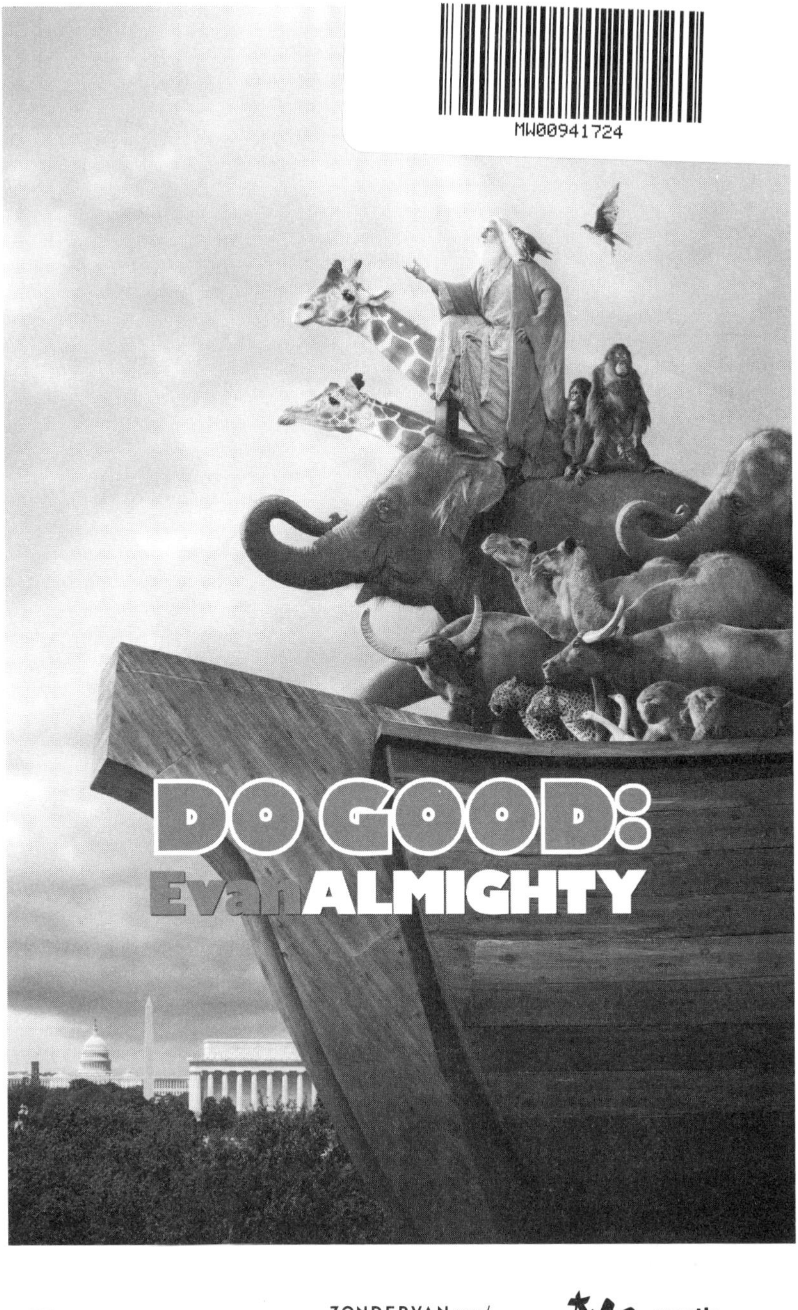

DO GOOD:
Evan ALMIGHTY

Do Good: Evan Almighty

Youth Specialties resources, 300 S. Pierce St., El Cajon, CA 92020 are published by Zondervan, 5300 Patterson Ave. SE, Grand Rapids, MI 49530.

Library of Congress Cataloging-in-Publication Data

Johnson, Kevin (Kevin Walter)
Do good : Evan Almighty / Kevin Johnson and Universal Studios.
p. cm.
Includes bibliographical references and index.
ISBN-10: 0-310-28414-7 (pbk. : alk. paper)
ISBN-13: 978-0-310-28414-7 (pbk. : alk. paper)
1. Teenagers—Religious life. 2. Teenagers—Conduct of life. 3. Caring—Religious aspects—Christianity. 4. Globalization—Religious aspects—Christianity. 5. Evan Almighty (Motion picture) I. Universal City Studios. II. Title.
BV4531.3.J643 2007
248.8'3—dc22

2007032194

Cover and interior design by David Conn

Printed in the United States of America

07 08 09 10 11 12 13 • 19 18 17 16 15 14 13 12 11 10 9 8 7 6 5 4 3 2 1

TO NATE, KARIN, AND ELISE

Go forth. Do good. Every chance you get.

TABLE OF CONTENTS

READ THIS FIRST

You might be stunned that a Hollywood blockbuster starring Steve Carell could alter your life, but *Evan Almighty* could do exactly that. The movie inspired this practical tool to help you change the world every chance you get—through simple, small, kind acts done right where you are, right now.

This journal is a companion to the *Evan Almighty Devotional*. You can work through this journal chapter by chapter as you go deep with that book or do this journal all by itself to grab ideas, energize your thoughts, and record your efforts to do good in the world. This journal will work well however you want to use it.

In this journal you'll find several key features:

- Each chapter contains **Quotes, Thoughts**, and **Questions** to jolt you to think and move you to act. (By the way, feel free to use a pen or pencil throughout this journal to scribble notes, thoughts, and answers to questions!)

- You'll see **Random Acts** at the bottom of each page. They're actions you can do almost anywhere, anytime, so flip through the journal to grab these instant ideas for making your world a better place.

- **Truth and Dare** invites you to get honest with how you might have acted in the past and choose to try something radically different. Scan for a truth that hits home with you, then do the dare.

- You'll also see pages titled **Random Act Note**. Just like Evan becomes part of an epic tale as God prompts him to do good, you'll construct your own amazing story as you act for good. Whenever you notice a need and do something about it, write about it on one of these pages. For more on how to uncover needs, you can bounce ahead to chapter 19 and learn about **Watch/Listen/Ask/Do/Repeat**.

God made you to do good, and you have the power to change the world one kind deed at a time. Read on—and never stop acting on what you discover.

CHAPTER 1

ROAD TRIP WITH JESUS

"Only a life lived for others is a life worthwhile."
—Albert Einstein (1879-1955), physicist

"Our prime purpose in this life is to help others. And if you can't help them, at least don't hurt them."
—Tenzin Gyatso (1935-), Tibetan Dalai Lama

Imagine standing on the white dotted line of a long desert highway that stretches like a ribbon to the horizon—an entirely traffic-free, silent scene. Your choice: Climb in your vehicle and drive forward or backward, on-road or off, down on the flats or up to the mountains. If you could just decide where you want to wind up at the end of the day, you'd know which route to take.

Jesus wants to nudge you toward what might be a new direction, a different destination. Doing so will get you traveling the same path he does, doing good with him wherever you can. The Bible says where he's headed, summed up in the words of one of his best friends: "You know what has happened all through the province of Judea…how God anointed Jesus of Nazareth with the Holy Spirit and power, and how he went around doing good..." (Acts 10:37). The Bible maps out your path when it says, "As God's chosen people, holy and dearly loved, clothe yourselves with compassion, kindness, humility, gentleness and patience" (Colossians 3:12).

This road trip with Jesus is pointless if it exists only in your imagination. It's all about your real, everyday actions—simple, small, kind acts, changing the world every chance you get, right where you are, right now.

What would you say is your largest purpose or goal in life?

How can you make a positive impact—either major or small—on your world?

Jesus said, "You didn't choose me, remember; I chose you, and put you in the world to bear fruit, fruit that won't spoil. As fruit bearers, whatever you ask the Father in relation to me, he gives you. But remember the root command: Love one another" (John 15:16-17 MSG).

How do you feel about the fact that God chose you to do good as one of your key tasks in life?

Where does loving others rank on your list of important things to do—high or low? What concrete proof do you have based on how you think, feel, and act?

TRUTH: Think about a time you and a friend ditched someone else.

DARE: Start a conversation with a person you usually avoid. Talk with that person for at least three minutes.

RANDOM ACT NOTE

"Wherever there is a human being,
there is an opportunity for kindness."
—Seneca (4 BC–AD 65), Roman philosopher

WATCH/LISTEN/ASK

A need I noticed...

DO

How I acted to meet the need...

REPEAT

How my deed turned out—and how I might do it differently next time...

CHAPTER 2

MAKE YOUR CHOICE

"No one can sum up all God is able to accomplish through one solitary life, wholly yielded, adjusted, and obedient to him."
—D.L. Moody (1837-1899), evangelist

"Today, even amongst Christians, there can be found much of that spirit that wants to give as little as possible to the Lord, and yet to get as much as possible from him...What he is after is that we pour all we have, ourselves, to him, and if that be all, that is enough."
—Watchman Nee (1903-1972), Chinese Christian martyr

From the first scene of *Evan Almighty* you can't help feeling a twinge of sympathy for Evan Baxter. Here's a guy striving to do good by serving his country as a congressman, but he never could have guessed that God Almighty would pop into his life and tell him to construct an ark (a la Noah from the Bible). Just as Evan is settling into a power-filled and predictable existence, God spins him off on an extraordinary adventure. If you haven't yet seen *Evan Almighty*, grab a look at the trailer online. You'll get the premise of the movie.

At first Evan hesitates when God tells him to construct a super-sized boat in several lots in his upscale neighborhood outside Washington, D.C. It's not giving away the plot to note that Evan finally gives in to God's grand plan. He decides to do the good thing God calls him to.

With that choice, Evan does exactly what Jesus did. Jesus came to earth wanting to do what God wanted, no matter what. He said it like this: "My food…is to do the will of him who sent me and to finish his work" (John 4:34). Following his Father's plan was so essential to Jesus that he called it his "food," the stuff he needed to survive.

While it's no secret that God wants us to obey him as eagerly as Evan—and Jesus—that's not always where we're at.

Why would Jesus say obeying God is so utterly important?

We're not Jesus, not the Son of God headed for the cross. More than a few thousand years ago, however, the Old Testament prophet Micah put down a short-and-sweet summary of God's plan for us: "He has shown all you people what is good. And what does the Lord require of you? To act justly and to love mercy and to walk humbly with your God" (Micah 6:8).

PARENTS ASK TWICE • ENROLL IN PEER-COUNSELING TRAINING • TREAT YOUR PARENTS TO

When does doing good—the way Micah describes it—come easy to you? When are you most unenthusiastic about those expectations?

There's no quick fix that'll make us instantly and always willing to do amazing good the way God wants us to, yet the starting point is talking to God. Invite him right now to impact how you think, feel, and act. Then tell him, "Here I am. Ready. Willing. Let's go."

RANDOM ACT NOTE

"Wherever there is a human being,
there is an opportunity for kindness."
—Seneca (4 BC–AD 65), Roman philosopher

WATCH/LISTEN/ASK

A need I noticed....

DO

How I acted to meet the need...

REPEAT

How my deed turned out—and how I might do it differently next time...

CHAPTER 3

THINGS THAT NEED FIXING

"The world is a dangerous place to live, not because of the people who are evil, but because of the people who don't do anything about it."

—Albert Einstein (1879-1955), physicist

"You must be the change you wish to see in the world."

—Mahatma Gandhi (1869-1948), father of India

If you are content with the world as it exists, then you might not be paying attention. While many of life's moments are bright and comfortable, it's no stretch to say that the world can be a tough place for any and all of us. Life is imperfect at best…frequently broken…sometimes completely shattered.

When we scan the planet we see environmental disasters, war, terrorism, disease, homelessness, racism, spiritual confusion, religious persecution, hunger, and slavery. We spot broken relationships, addictions, abuse, financial distress, loneliness, depression, and disabilities.

The question isn't whether problems exist; it's whether we're willing to face them and do something about them.

No one likes to climb out of his comfort bubble and gaze at the pain all around us. Yet that's what Jesus did. He left the bright shining glory of heaven to be born on earth as a human being. John 1:14 says, "The Word became flesh and made his dwelling among us." He saw evil up close yet refused to take part. He knew its impact on the whole human race and came determined to do something about it.

What problems far and near most trouble you?

It doesn't take an Einstein to notice that evil abounds. Yet how bad is it if you see suffering you could ease or simple opportunities to boost someone's day—yet do nothing? Check James 4:17 for an answer.

THE FIGHT AGAINST HUNGER • TEACH SOMEONE OLDER HOW TO USE EMAIL OR IM OR TEXT • PICK

Jesus could have written off humankind; he was in no way the cause of our issues. But he didn't. How do you, like Jesus, fight the attitude that if something bad isn't happening to you, then it's not your problem?

TRUTH: Think about something you've posted online about yourself that isn't true.

DARE: Fix your online fictions this week.

RANDOM ACT NOTE

"Wherever there is a human being,
there is an opportunity for kindness."
—Seneca (4 BC–AD 65), Roman philosopher

WATCH/LISTEN/ASK

A need I noticed....

DO

How I acted to meet the need...

REPEAT

How my deed turned out—and how I might do it differently next time...

COUPONS • ORDER (AND PAY FOR) PIZZA FOR YOUR FAMILY • PICK UP A NEIGHBOR'S MAIL •

CHAPTER 4

GIVE LIFE

"We live in ignorance of the wealth of love that God has for us."
—Rich Mullins (1955-1997), Christian singer-songwriter

"No kind action ever stops with itself. One kind action leads to another. Good example is followed. A single act of kindness throws out roots in all directions, and the roots spring up and make new trees. The greatest work that kindness does to others is that it makes them kind themselves."
—Amelia Earhart (1897-1939), aviator

God designed a perfect world. Though it's tough to swallow, humankind has made our imperfect, broken, shattered planet what it is. Yet right from the start, God has had a plan to remake the world.

It's true that God loves us just the way we are. After all, while we were still a sinful mess, Jesus died for us (Romans 5:8). Yet God also loves us too much to leave us this way. When Jesus arrived, he came bearing freedom for prisoners, sight for the blind, good news for the poor, freedom for the oppressed, God's favor for all (Luke 4:18-19). Or like he said, "I came to give life—life in all its fullness" (John 10:10).

Despite what many people think about him, God wishes the best for every human being and for every facet of life. He wants us to grasp the mind-boggling intensity of his love for us. Look at what the apostle Paul prayed for some young Christians: "May you have the power to understand, as all God's people should, how wide, how long, how high, and how deep his love is. May you experience the love of Christ, though it is too great to understand fully. Then you will be made complete with all the fullness of life and power that comes from God" (Ephesians 3:18-19 NLT).

If you get hold of that kind of love from God, you can't help but want to give it away to people all around you. You can get on board with God's grand plan to remake the world.

What have humans messed up from God's original design for our world? Or what bad things do you think God wants to see fixed?

How do you see God's goodness in your life? What all does he do for you?

Maybe it's tough for you to answer the previous question. Look at what James 1:17 says, then add to your list: "Whatever is good and perfect comes down to us from God our Father, who created all the lights in the heavens. He never changes or casts a shifting shadow" (NLT). You can look at Psalm 145:14-19 and Romans 8:38-39 for even more details about God's nonstop love.

What does receiving God's love, kindness, and mercy have to do with the ability to pass it on?

RANDOM ACT NOTE

"Wherever there is a human being,
there is an opportunity for kindness."
—Seneca (4 BC–AD 65), Roman philosopher

WATCH/LISTEN/ASK

A need I noticed....

DO

How I acted to meet the need...

REPEAT

How my deed turned out—and how I might do it differently next time...

CHAPTER 5

ADMIT EVIL

"Sin is not to be ignored, nor minimized. It is the most patent fact in life, the darkest experience in the history of the race. It is the root of all the world's tragedies."
—James Mann Campbell (1840-1926), author

"You may have a fresh start any moment you choose, for this thing that we call 'failure' is not the falling down, but the staying down."
—Mary Pickford (1893-1979), Canadian actress

So this guy claiming to be God Almighty shows up and claims a flood is coming. He helps himself to a spot in the backseat of Evan's Hummer. He pops up in Evan's driveway. He causes every strain of critter to flock around Evan everywhere he goes. And he tells Evan to build an ark.

Evan says, "This conversation is a little thing I like to call 'over.'"

We might have the same no-way, no-how reaction to God's commands. After all, who is this guy telling us to do good? He's the one who bounced Adam and Eve from their home in paradise, the Garden of Eden (Genesis 3:1-24). He's the all-powerful being who declared, "I will completely wipe out this human race that I have created" (Genesis 6:7, NLT), then sent a flood upon the earth. What lesson can we learn about doing good from a God like that?

What we can learn from these episodes is the true awfulness of sin. God was so brokenhearted by nonstop human sin that he had to put an end to it (Genesis 6:5-6). Even a fresh start after Noah and the flood wasn't enough to exterminate sin, which set the stage for God's ultimate, world-changing gift: Jesus.

Read these statements and indicate if you agree or disagree and why:

A good God doesn't create human beings who have no choice but to obey him—so he gave us freedom to pick right or wrong.

Agree? Disagree? Why?

A good God won't let evil go unchecked—if he did, we would judge him an unfair, uncaring monster.

Agree? Disagree? Why?

A great God also doesn't give up on the world he loves—so in time he reveals the plan he's concocted to rescue and remake us.

Agree? Disagree? Why?

Of all that the Bible says about sin, here are three prime verses: "We all, like sheep, have gone astray, each of us has turned to our own way" (Isaiah 53:6); "Everyone has sinned and fallen short of God's glorious standard" (Romans 3:23 NCV); "If we claim to be without sin, we deceive ourselves and the truth is not in us" (1 John 1:8).

If you were God, how would you solve the problem of human evil?

TRUTH: Recall a time you did something wrong but got away with it.

DARE: Figure out a way to make up for what you did—and do it.

RANDOM ACT NOTE

"Wherever there is a human being,
there is an opportunity for kindness."
—Seneca (4 BC–AD 65), Roman philosopher

WATCH/LISTEN/ASK

A need I noticed....

DO

How I acted to meet the need...

REPEAT

How my deed turned out—and how I might do it differently next time...

SOMEONE ELSE GO FIRST • SIT BY THE NEW KID • SPLIT A DESSERT • GREET PEOPLE • HOLD A

CHAPTER 6

BE THE MASTERPIECE

"Sad will be the day for any man when he becomes contented with the thoughts he is thinking and the deeds he is doing—where there is not forever beating at the doors of his soul some great desire to do something larger; which he knows he was meant and made to do."
—Phillips Brooks (1835-1893), Episcopal bishop

"Whatever you are, be a good one."
—Abraham Lincoln (1809-1865), U.S. president

There's a scene in the middle of the Old Testament where the prophet Samuel hunts for a king to rule God's people. God sends him to a man, Jesse, who lines up his sons, starting with the oldest. Just like the proud dad hopes, Samuel is impressed by the bearing and stature of the oldest son. But God whispers, "That's not the one." Actually, he says, "Do not consider his appearance or his height, for I have rejected him. The Lord does not look at the things human beings look at. People look at the outward appearance, but the Lord looks at the heart" (1 Samuel 16:7). The prophet sees each son in turn until no one is left.

It's a Cinderella moment, because there's one more son—the youngest, David. He's tending sheep, the family's grunt job, dangerous and lonely. When Jesse calls David from the fields, he's the one God chooses to be king.

Learn from David: People might not take you seriously, but God does. Some might think you're clueless; God says you're capable. The Bible says, "For we are God's masterpiece. He has created us anew in Christ Jesus, so we can do the good things he planned for us long ago" (Ephesians 2:10 NLT1996). In this context, *masterpiece* means "handiwork" or "workmanship" or even "poem." When God looks at you, he sees his own handcrafted, perfect work of art.

God didn't just have a plan for David; God has one for you as well. You're his hand-picked choice. He has a plan for you to do good. There's no doubt about it, because he mapped out your path a long time ago.

Think about this: Within you is a unique assortment of God-given gifts, quirks, and challenges that make you a one-of-a-kind agent for change. Your talents, personality, spiritual gifts, values, and passions add up to abilities no one else has to meet needs all around you.

God gave you gifts that are useful for doing good in the world. What are yours?

If you're not sure how to answer that question, scan the Random Acts list running along the bottoms of the pages in this book. Which are you really good at?

Who in your world takes you seriously? How do you feel when they show you respect?

What good does it do you to know that God calls you his masterpiece?

EACH WEEK • BE VULNERABLE • INVITE SOMEONE TO A PARTY • GIVE A GREEN (ENERGY-

RANDOM ACT NOTE

"Wherever there is a human being,
there is an opportunity for kindness."
—Seneca (4 BC–AD 65), Roman philosopher

WATCH/LISTEN/ASK

A need I noticed....

DO

How I acted to meet the need...

REPEAT

How my deed turned out—and how I might do it differently next time...

EFFICIENT) LIGHT BULB TO EVERYONE ON YOUR BLOCK • PLAY CATCH WITH A YOUNGER KID •

CHAPTER 7

GO CRAZY

"Make thee an ark of gopher wood; rooms shalt thou make in the ark, and shalt pitch it within and without with pitch."
—God to Noah (Genesis 6:14 KJV)

"I want to know all God's thoughts; all the rest are just details."
—Albert Einstein (1879-1955), physicist

Noah probably didn't know anything more about building a 450-foot long ark than you do. The Bible doesn't mention that he had an oceanfront beach house or ran a multinational shipbuilding business. Yet God thought nothing of telling this guy and his family to construct a boat one-and-a-half football fields long. And if Evan Baxter were a real person, we'd have even more reason to wonder about the Almighty's instructions.

The Bible cautions us that we won't always grasp all of God's logic. As long as we act as though sin's a good idea, God says to us, "For my thoughts are not your thoughts, neither are your ways my ways" (Isaiah 55:8). He hints that our own insights can be inadequate: "Trust in the Lord with all your heart and lean not on your own understanding; in all your ways submit to him, and he will make your paths straight" (Proverbs 3:5-6).

But don't assume our imperfect understanding of God's reasoning means God doesn't have reasons for what he does. As you flip through Scripture you see that God tells multiple individuals to do seemingly crazy things—nothing as reckless as what you can catch on YouTube, but quirky nonetheless. You don't have to dig far into these accounts, however, to see that there's a levelheaded message or purpose behind the commands. For instance, when God tells the prophet Hosea to marry a prostitute—a deed that demonstrates God's constant love for his unfaithful people (Hosea 1:2-3). Or when Esther the Queen obeys God and risks her life to save her people, an act that ensures her character is as regal as her beauty (Esther 4:12-14).

Despite these somewhat strange commands, the *what* and *why* of most of God's instructions are obvious. Even so, do you believe God always has a good reason for his commands? Why—or why not?

The only thing worse than obeying a seemingly crazy command is obeying because you feel threatened or forced into compliance. We can do good because we have to, but it's not much fun. Even God isn't excited about forced obedience. Instead he aims to motivate us from the inside—so we do good because *want* to.

Ponder this quote from Gregory of Nazianzus (329-389), Bishop of Constantinople, and write down what you think it means: "The mystery of godliness belongs to those who are willing, not to those who are overpowered."

TRUTH: Recall a time when you put yourself and others at risk by showing off while driving.

DARE: Drive for the next week with music off, phone hung up, both hands on the wheel, and under the speed limit.

RANDOM ACT NOTE

"Wherever there is a human being,
there is an opportunity for kindness."
—Seneca (4 BC–AD 65), Roman philosopher

WATCH/LISTEN/ASK

A need I noticed....

DO

How I acted to meet the need...

REPEAT

How my deed turned out—and how I might do it differently next time...

PRINT IT, FRAME IT, GIVE IT • GIVE CHIP CLIPS TO YOUR WHOLE BLOCK • CAMPAIGN FOR A

CHAPTER 8

GO CRAZY REDUX

"I find that doing of the will of God leaves me no time for disputing about His plans."
—George MacDonald (1824-1905), Scottish novelist

"Let this be your whole endeavor, this your prayer, this your desire—that you may be stripped of all selfishness, and with entire simplicity follow Jesus only."
—Thomas à Kempis (1380–1471), Christian monk

Think about everything you know about how God wants you to live—the right and wrong things you know in your gut as well as the dos and don'ts you read in the Bible. Now answer this: Which of God's expectations feel especially unreasonable?

It's probably not "You shall not murder" (Exodus 20:13). Most of us are okay with that one. Ditto for "You shall not commit adultery" (20:14). But we might fudge on not lying (20:16), always honoring Mom and Dad (20:12), or coveting a neighbor's new game system and jumbo-screen HDTV (20:17). If we have trouble totally agreeing with some of God's top-10 commandments, we won't do any better when we get to the rest.

Human beings naturally dodge the full scope of God's commands. Example: "Imitate God, therefore, in everything you do, because you are his dear children. Live a life filled with love, following the example of Christ. He loved us and offered himself as a sacrifice for us" (Ephesians 5:1-2). Imitate God? Sacrifice and love just like Jesus? Both are laughably enormous, feats totally impossible without God's help.

But stop laughing and think hard about this. If you really want to do good in this world, you need to come to a moment when your view of God's expectations undergoes a significant shift. You stop doubting God and start trusting. You quit thinking "God must be crazy!" and come to an outrageously different conclusion: "God knows what he's doing!" That's when following Jesus becomes your endeavor, your prayer, and your desire. You choose to do what God wants you to do.

Put your answer in writing: Which of God's commands seem most unworkable to you? What does God expect of you that you wish he didn't?

So what do you do when following God seems crazy? When have you talked honestly with God about what he expects of you?

We need God's reassurance that his commands have real benefits for us and our world. He gives it to us in Psalm 19: "The teachings of the Lord are perfect; they give new strength. The rules of the Lord can be trusted; they make plain people wise. The orders of the Lord are right; they make people happy. The commands of the Lord are pure; they light up the way. Respect for the Lord is good; it will last forever. The judgments of the Lord are true; they are completely right" (Psalm 19:7-9 NCV).

How much do you agree with all of that? Tell God what you think.

TRUTH: Think of a task you always weasel out of at home or work.

DARE: Do that task without being asked this week. At least twice.

RANDOM ACT NOTE

"Wherever there is a human being,
there is an opportunity for kindness."
—Seneca (4 BC–AD 65), Roman philosopher

WATCH/LISTEN/ASK

A need I noticed....

DO

How I acted to meet the need...

REPEAT

How my deed turned out—and how I might do it differently next time...

CHAPTER 9

SERVE

"The true meaning of life is to plant trees, under whose shade you do not expect to sit."
—Nelson Henderson

"Love is unselfishly choosing for another's highest good."
—C. S. Lewis (1898-1963), Christian author

Picture your school lunchroom with its astonishing assortment of people, then picture yourself putting every word of this passage into action: "When you do things, do not let selfishness or pride be your guide. Instead, be humble and give more honor to others than to yourselves. Do not be interested only in your own life, but be interested in the lives of others. In your lives you must think and act like Christ Jesus" (Philippians 2:3-5 NCV).

Does that actually work in your lunchroom? Or the science lab? Or the football field?

When you get right down to it, that's strange stuff. Putting aside self-centeredness. Valuing others. Watching out not just for yourself but for others. You could argue that such radically unselfish attitudes and actions are weirder than building an ark. It's maybe the craziest command in the whole Bible.

Even Jesus' closest disciples struggled to understand this kind of servanthood. They saw it every day in their master, but they still argued about which one of them would be the greatest when Jesus came back to rule in blazing glory. But Jesus silenced them: "Whoever wants to become great among you must be your servant, and whoever wants to be first must be your slave—just as the Son of Man did not come to be served, but to serve, and to give his life as a ransom for many" (Matthew 20:26-28).

If you want to follow Jesus, you get to be like him, a servant who pours out all. It's your chance to change the world—even when it seems crazy.

What does doing good have to do with being a servant? Can you do one without the other?

When have you served others? How did it turn out? What was the toughest part—and the best?

Agree—or disagree—and explain your response: Being a servant isn't for everyone.

TRUTH: Think about something you own that you hate to share.

DARE: Give someone a turn with your prized possession this week.

RANDOM ACT NOTE

"Wherever there is a human being,
there is an opportunity for kindness."
—Seneca (4 BC–AD 65), Roman philosopher

WATCH/LISTEN/ASK

A need I noticed….

DO

How I acted to meet the need…

REPEAT

How my deed turned out—and how I might do it differently next time…

FRIEND A CAR WASH • BRING GARBAGE CANS UP FROM THE CURB • DISTRACT BULLIES • WRITE A

CHAPTER 10

GO SMALL

"Great acts are made up of small deeds."
—Lao Tzu (6th century BC), Chinese philosopher

"Nobody made a greater mistake than he who did nothing because he could only do a little."
—Edmund Burke (1729-1797), Anglo-Irish statesman

Maybe you have an amazing dream of doing good. You might want to halt global warming. To usher in world peace. To solve poverty, the AIDS crisis, slavery, or sex trafficking. You might want to ensure that people all around the globe enjoy an eternal destiny with God.

God has some big dreams for you, his masterpiece. His dreams stretch to the end of the planet and span as long as you live and breathe.

But there's a key to his dreams worth remembering: God's plans for you never ignore where you are, right now. He packs every moment with opportunities to do good for your family, strangers seated next to you at school, and neighbors down the block and around your community.

Don't ever let go of a single giant dream. But your monumental visions aren't where you start doing good; you need a "now-sized" view of your task.

Here it is: "Small is the new big."

When you first begin to purposely, consciously engage in doing good, don't let your focus drift to the gargantuan unless it's to decide on a bite-sized piece. For now, think small. Brainstorm something you can do in the next hour or two. Or the next day or two. If you really aspire to do an act of kindness that needs a week or two (or more) to plan and carry out, then start mulling what smaller deeds you can do in the meantime.

Every small act makes a big difference in someone's life, because it does real good right here, right now.

Do you really believe God cares about you doing little good acts? Why—or why not?

How can doing a small act start something big?

GRANDPARENTS TO A PARK • CRANK UP A SNOWCONE MACHINE IN YOUR NEIGHBORHOOD • MAKE

When have you seen a small kind act make a big impact on someone's life?

A lot can happen in a day. What small things could you do in the next 24 hours to make someone's world better?

RANDOM ACT NOTE

"Wherever there is a human being,
there is an opportunity for kindness."
—Seneca (4 BC–AD 65), Roman philosopher

WATCH/LISTEN/ASK

A need I noticed....

DO

How I acted to meet the need...

REPEAT

How my deed turned out—and how I might do it differently next time...

HIGH-FIVE AN ELEPHANT • COMPLIMENT SOMEONE'S OUTFIT • GIVE FAST FOOD GIFT CERTIFICATES

CHAPTER 11

GO BEYOND GOOD INTENTIONS

"The smallest good deed is better than the grandest intention."
—*Jacques-Joseph Duguet (1649-1733), theologian*

"Sometimes we just need a firm kick in the pants. An unsmiling expectation that if we mean all these wonderful things we talk about and sing about, then let's see something to prove it."
—*Dietrich Bonhoeffer (1906-1945), German Christian martyr* *

It's the thought that counts.

Or maybe not.

If a thought never turns into a deed, it's all intention and no action. And that's not doing good.

The Bible says that actually acting for good is evidence that our faith is genuine. The apostle James offers an example: "What good is it, my brothers and sisters, if people claim to have faith but have no deeds? Can such faith save them? Suppose a brother or sister is without clothes and daily food. If one of you says to them, 'Go in peace; keep warm and well fed,' but does nothing about their physical needs, what good is it?" (James 2:14-16).

Spiritual poseurs forget that real faith demonstrates itself through action. It's a sure test of whether we're acting for good—or just thinking about acting for good. It's possible to look concerned, gush with emotion, talk a lot, and even buy the correct T-shirt without accomplishing anything solid.

Doing good is more than thinking about change, desiring better things for someone, or wishing the world were different. It's about doing whatever small things you can right here, right now—serving others, putting someone else before yourself, committing random acts of kindness.

When you've done good for someone else, you know it. You see a concrete result. You've proven what you claim to believe.

What do you think—is it "the thought that counts"? Why—or why not?

When have you seen people say they're concerned about the world's ills but do nothing? (Make sure your first example is about yourself.)

How do you want to bust out of "all intention and no action"? What kindness can you do within the next hour to actually accomplish some small measure of goodness?

* Dietrich Bonhoeffer was a prominent German theologian hanged by the Nazis shortly before the end of World War II for his efforts to defend Jews and plot the downfall of Adolf Hitler. Definitely not a spiritual poseur, he left behind deep writings on what it means to truly follow Jesus. His best known work is *The Cost of Discipleship*, a book he wrote during Hitler's rise to power.

TRUTH: Think about a time you told your parents you were going someplace—but went somewhere else instead. Or with somebody—but with someone else instead.

DARE: Keep your word to your parents this week.

RANDOM ACT NOTE

"Wherever there is a human being,
there is an opportunity for kindness."
—Seneca (4 BC–AD 65), Roman philosopher

WATCH/LISTEN/ASK

A need I noticed....

DO

How I acted to meet the need...

REPEAT

How my deed turned out—and how I might do it differently next time...

SIBLING SHOPPING • TALK TO SOMEONE WHO'S USUALLY LEFT OUT • VOLUNTEER AT YOUR OLD

CHAPTER 12

DON'T STOP

"Let the professors of Christianity recommend their religion by deeds of benevolence—by Christian meekness—by lives of temperance and holiness."
—*Richard Mentor Johnson (1780-1850), U.S. vice president*

"He who governed the world before I was born shall take care of it likewise when I am dead. My part is to improve the present moment."
—*John Wesley (1703–1791), evangelist and theologian*

Doing good isn't just for mothers—or just for pastors, Sunday school teachers, and peers without much of a life. Doing good is a core task for every Christian.

Acting for good might feel like all those activities you signed up for when you were little. You might have jumped into baseball...or dance...scouting...softball...art classes... piano lessons...soccer...or a mess of other pursuits. After a while, however, you figure out what's your thing and what's not. Your parents might sigh with disappointment when you drop something you've been pursuing in favor of something else, but the world doesn't stop turning. In hindsight, what looked like a must-do turned out to be something you could quit with few consequences.

But doing good isn't one of those activities you can ditch at will. Acting for good is central to what God is up to in the world—and to what he wants us to be about.

Look at just a few of the places the Bible says this directly: "Trust in the Lord and do good" (Psalm 37:3); "I know that there is nothing better for people than to be happy and to do good while they live" (Ecclesiastes 3:12); "Do not forget to do good and to share with others, for with such sacrifices God is pleased" (Hebrews 13:16).

Remember—you are God's masterpiece. He created you anew in Christ Jesus so you can do the good things he planned for you long ago (Ephesians 2:10). If you're not learning to act for good, you're not giving away the love you've received from God. And you're missing out on what you're made for.

When has doing good felt like an optional extra?

What convinces you that doing good isn't something you can let slide?

There's a practical issue in all of this: You can't help everyone in the world or make even a tiny dent in every problem. So how do you know when it's time to stop doing good?

TRUTH: Recall the most recent occasion you mouthed off to a parent, teacher, or other adult.

DARE: Come up with your own kind deed to do for that person.

RANDOM ACT NOTE

"Wherever there is a human being,
there is an opportunity for kindness."
—Seneca (4 BC–AD 65), Roman philosopher

WATCH/LISTEN/ASK

A need I noticed....

DO

How I acted to meet the need...

REPEAT

How my deed turned out—and how I might do it differently next time...

CHAPTER 13

DO WHAT YOU KNOW

"He who sees a need and waits to be asked for help is as unkind as if he had refused it."
—Dante Alighieri (1265–1321), Italian poet

"Talking isn't doing. It is a kind of good deed to say well; and yet words are not deeds."
—William Shakespeare (1564-1616), English poet and playwright

---

Evan spouts off when God says he wants him to build an ark:

"This conversation is a little thing I like to call 'over.' SHEEP!"

God assumes he has the right guy. Having campaigned on the theme of "Think Big, Think Baxter, and Change the World!" Evan appears to be someone who wants to do good. But a boat stuffed to the gills with critters doesn't exactly fit Evan's plan to be successful...powerful...handsome...happy. When it comes to obeying God's command, he stalls.

We can't claim we're accomplishing anything good if we merely hear God's call and do nothing about it. In fact, when we come to understand all that God has to say about doing good and yet stay unengaged, we're acting downright ridiculous. Here's how the book of James puts it: "Those who listen to the word but do not do what it says are like people who look at their faces in a mirror and, after looking at themselves, go away and immediately forget what they look like" (James 1:23-24).

There's a solution to that—and it's not continuing to shoot your nostrils full of shaving cream to get rid of your nose hairs. It's about doing something—anything—not just to look good but to actually do good. James 1:22 couldn't make it any clearer: "Do not merely listen to the word, and so deceive yourselves. Do what it says."

When have you totally ignored God's call to do good—maybe not an assignment to build an ark, but something really obvious that you knew you should do?

If you had a chance to rewind that scene, would you act differently now? Why—or why not?

Put it in your own words: Why is it so ludicrous to know the right thing to do yet not do it?

Now that you know all this stuff about doing good, are you ready to tell God that you want to be his agent for good in the world? You don't have to use those exact words, but what do you want to tell him right now?

TRUTH: Think of something you "borrowed" and haven't returned.

DARE: Give the item back to its owner this week.

RANDOM ACT NOTE

"Wherever there is a human being,
there is an opportunity for kindness."
—Seneca (4 BC–AD 65), Roman philosopher

WATCH/LISTEN/ASK

A need I noticed....

DO

How I acted to meet the need...

REPEAT

How my deed turned out—and how I might do it differently next time...

A BACKYARD CARNIVAL • FIX A CAR • PUT TOGETHER A PHOTO ALBUM (FEATURING PHOTOS OF

CHAPTER 14

STAND ALONE

"People tend to want to follow the beaten path. The difficulty is that the beaten path doesn't seem to be leading anywhere."
—Charles Mathias (1922-), U.S. senator

"Cowardice asks the question: Is it safe?
Expediency asks the question: Is it politic?
Vanity asks the question: Is it popular?
But conscience asks the question: Is it right?
And there comes a time when one must take a position that is neither safe, nor politic, nor popular—but one must take it simply because it is right."
—Martin Luther King, Jr. (1929-1968), civil rights leader

Evan Baxter has a boatload of animals chasing him down, but he doesn't find many takers to help him in his God-assigned task. Yet he chooses to change the world even when standing alone.

Jesus is the supreme real-life example of this gutsy attitude. On the night he was betrayed with a kiss to those in power who wanted him dead, Jesus knew his 12 closest followers would abandon him. "This very night," he predicts, "you will all fall away on account of me, for it is written: 'I will strike the shepherd, and the sheep of the flock will be scattered'" (Matthew 26:27).

The circumstances come to pass just as Jesus predicts. As he prays in the Garden of Gethsemane hours before his arrest, his three best friends—Peter, James, and John—doze off instead of staying awake to pray with him (Matthew 26:36-46). He was sold out to the authorities by one of his 12 disciples—Judas Iscariot (Matthew 26:47-50). Three times Peter says he doesn't know Jesus (Matthew 26:69-74). At the cross we see only John, Mary the mother of Jesus, and a few women who watch from a distance (Matthew 27:55-56; John 19:25-27).

Even though Jesus stands alone, he doesn't veer from his determination to change the world. The Bible says we should be encouraged by this: "Consider him who endured such opposition from sinners, so that you will not grow weary and lose heart" (Hebrews 12:3). The one who stands alone can teach us to stay strong even when no one stands with us.

When have you experienced pressure that held you back from doing good?

How have you chosen to do right despite what others say?

What keeps you motivated to do good? How do you stay eager to be part of God's plan?

TRUTH: Think of a time you were part of a group that was making fun of someone.

DARE: Make a card for the person you mocked—and deliver it by hand.

RANDOM ACT NOTE

"Wherever there is a human being,
there is an opportunity for kindness."
—Seneca (4 BC–AD 65), Roman philosopher

WATCH/LISTEN/ASK

A need I noticed....

DO

How I acted to meet the need...

REPEAT

How my deed turned out—and how I might do it differently next time...

SCRUB TOYS IN THE CHURCH NURSERY • CLEAN UP GRAFFITI • MAKE A MEAL FOR A SICK

CHAPTER 15

STAND TOGETHER

"Never doubt that a small group of thoughtful, committed citizens can change the world. Indeed, it's the only thing that ever has."

—Margaret Mead (1901-1978), anthropologist

"The level of our obedience is most often determined by the behavior standard of other Christians around us."

—Jerry Bridges (1929-), Christian author

Titus worked in a tough neighborhood. Not any place you would recognize, but a mountainous island in the south of Greece. Not long after Jesus died and rose again, Titus took a job as a pastor on Crete. The thugs who lived there—the Cretans—were so well known for their blatant deceit that all around their Mediterranean world the verb "to Cretanize" was the equivalent of "to lie." In a short note to Titus, the apostle Paul quotes Crete's most famous poet, who had nothing nice to say about his own people. Says Epimenides: "Cretans are always liars, evil brutes, lazy gluttons" (Titus 1:12).

Paul adds some instructions for Titus to pass on to the believers. He says, “Remind the people to be subject to rulers and authorities, to be obedient, to be ready to do whatever is good, to slander no one, to be peaceable and considerate, and always to be gentle toward everyone” (Titus 3:1-2).

Taking Paul's advice might sound like a sure way to get slugged, but the point is that God wants these believers to act for good in a society even more dishonest, brutal, and selfish than the one we live in. He expects them to band together, to take a stand together for right.

When have you seen pressure from others become a positive thing?

Who helps you do good when everyone around you is being bad?

Hebrews 10:24 says, "Think of ways to encourage one another to outbursts of love and good deeds" (NLT 1996). The word *encourage* literally means to "irritate" or "exasperate." The goal isn't to annoy one another but to inspire and motivate each other to care intensely for other people and for our world.

How can you and your friends help each other toward outbursts of good deeds?

TRUTH: Think about a time you duped your parents by changing your clothes, hair, or makeup between home and school.

DARE: Go to school all week looking like you do when you hug your mom and dad goodbye.

RANDOM ACT NOTE

"Wherever there is a human being,
there is an opportunity for kindness."
—Seneca (4 BC–AD 65), Roman philosopher

WATCH/LISTEN/ASK

A need I noticed....

DO

How I acted to meet the need...

REPEAT

How my deed turned out—and how I might do it differently next time...

ENGLISH • GIVE YOUR MOM A HUG • WRAP A GIFT • PLAN AN OUTING WITH SOMEONE ON THE

CHAPTER 16

DITCH SIN

"The reason for not going out and sinning all you like is the same as the reason for not going out and putting your nose in a slicing machine: It's dumb, stupid, and no fun... Betrayal, jealousy, love grown cold, and the gray dawn of the morning after are nobody's idea of a good time."
—Robert Farrar Capon (1925-), Episcopal priest and author

"Sin is not hurtful because it is forbidden, but it is forbidden because it is hurtful."
—Benjamin Franklin (1706-1790), American founding father and statesman

---

Every time you do wrong, you believe you're making a brilliant choice.

Maybe saying it like that is too blunt. But the truth is that whenever we do a bad thing, something in our heads tells us it's a better choice than doing good.

You can spot this phenomenon all the way back in the Garden of Eden, that episode where Adam and Eve eat forbidden fruit from the tree of the knowledge of good and evil. Coached by a smooth-talking serpent, the world's first couple concludes that their leap into evil is the correct choice. They begin by misinterpreting God's rule, making it stricter than God himself says. (In Genesis 3:3 Eve says that God banned touching the fruit, contradicting the real command in Genesis 2:17, which was simply to not eat.) They doubt the consequences of doing evil (3:4). Then they question God's total goodness, concluding he's withholding something good from them (3:5).

Doing evil always lures us with a promise of something good for us. As the ancient Greek philosopher Plato writes, "Pleasure is the bait of sin."

If you want to act for good in this world, you must be absolutely convinced that bad is never a brilliant choice. Not only that, but persuaded that any sin that Jesus had to die for is worth tossing from your life. Having that accurate view of evil is the first step to throwing off "everything that hinders" and "the sin that so easily entangles" (Hebrews 12:1) so you can do the deeds God planned for you long ago.

Why is sin so appealing to us?

How can you get an accurate view of the badness of any kind of wrongdoing?

How convinced are you that any sin bad enough to send Jesus to the cross is also bad enough to toss from your life?

God wants us to get up and move forward when we fail in our efforts to do life his way. He also wants us to know how simple it is to get a fresh start whenever we need it: "If we confess our sins, he is faithful and just and will forgive us our sins and purify us from all unrighteousness. If we claim we have not sinned, we make him out to be a liar and his word is not in us" (1 John 1:9-10).

RANDOM ACT NOTE

"Wherever there is a human being,
there is an opportunity for kindness."
—*Seneca (4 BC–AD 65), Roman philosopher*

WATCH/LISTEN/ASK

A need I noticed....

DO

How I acted to meet the need...

REPEAT

How my deed turned out—and how I might do it differently next time...

(USE COMMON SENSE AND BE SAFE: GO WITH FRIENDS OR TAKE AN ADULT, AND DON'T GO AT NIGHT)

CHAPTER 17

STAY STRONG

"It is curious that physical courage should be so common in the world and moral courage so rare."
—Mark Twain (1835-1920), humorist and author

"Great deeds are usually wrought at great risks."
—Herodotus (484 BC–ca. 425 BC), Greek historian

If you have to die, a cross isn't the way you want to go. Practiced by the Romans throughout their empire, crucifixion was preceded by scourging with whips embedded with bone and metal. Nailing the victim's wrists to T-shaped wooden beams caused unbearable pain, but crucifixion ultimately caused death by suffocation because a victim could only catch his breath by pushing upward against nailed-pierced feet.

Crucifixion was Rome's most severe form of execution, and the Jews regarded it the most hideous form of death possible. And yet all of this physical suffering doesn't begin to compare to the spiritual thrashing Jesus endured as he died for the world's sins.

But check out how Jesus viewed his crucifixion: "For

the joy set before him he endured the cross, scorning its shame, and sat down at the right hand of the throne of God" (Hebrews 12:2). "Scorning its shame" means Jesus paid so little attention to the emotional humiliation, physical pain, and spiritual agony of the cross that he didn't bother to dodge it. On the far side of the cross he saw the chance to win salvation for a world he loves. The anticipated results of his pain brought him indescribable joy.

When acting for good causes you pain, look ahead to the results your actions will bring. It's okay to count the costs, but you'll gain courage when you add up the benefits. After prayer and God's grace, that's how you get strength to change the world—even when doing good gets difficult.

When have you tried to do good, but it got so hard you just had to quit?

What's the most you've ever sacrificed? What good did it do?

What difficult task do you face right now? What good will result if you go ahead with your deed?

TRUTH: Remember a prank you pulled on a cranky neighbor.

DARE: Do something unexpectedly kind for that cranky neighbor.

RANDOM ACT NOTE

"Wherever there is a human being,
there is an opportunity for kindness."
—Seneca (4 BC–AD 65), Roman philosopher

WATCH/LISTEN/ASK

A need I noticed....

DO

How I acted to meet the need…

REPEAT

How my deed turned out—and how I might do it differently next time…

ETC.) • GIVE AWAY HOT CHOCOLATE OR COFFEE ON A COLD DAY • RAKE LEAVES • HELP YOUR

CHAPTER 18

STEP UP

"To fight evil one must also recognize one's own responsibility. The values for which we stand must be expressed in the way we think of, and how we deal with, our fellow humans."

—Beatrix of the Netherlands (1938-), Queen Regnant of the Kingdom

"No one would remember the Good Samaritan if he'd only had good intentions— he had money, too."

—Margaret Thatcher (1925-), prime minister of the United Kingdom

---

"Put your money where your mouth is."

That's exactly what the individual known as "the Good Samaritan" did. Unlike two religious leaders who walked by the mugging victim they saw lying on the side of a road, the man Jesus describes in Luke 10:30-37 bandaged the dying stranger, took him to shelter, nursed him to health, then sacrificed his own money to the mugging victim's ongoing care.

Every day you stumble across people who need your help. Lending a hand isn't solely about giving money—but it does mean jumping in wherever you can.

You might have dreams of doing good for people all over this planet. Don't ever let go of those dreams, and do them as large as you can. But you are God's indispensable plan for helping people within your immediate reach. So it's never okay to say you want to help people far away if you neglect the ones nearby. Or to claim you love God if you don't care for the people you see every day. Changing your world starts right here, right now, right under your nose.

The great Methodist preacher John Wesley (1703-1791) sums it up: "Do all the good you can, by all the means you can, in all the ways you can, in all the places you can, at all the times you can, to all the people you can, as long as ever you can." U.S. President Teddy Roosevelt (1858-1919) drives home the same point through a slogan tight enough to fit on a sticky note inside your locker: "Do what you can, with what you have, where you are."

Who do you know who needs your help right now—physical assistance, homework help, emotional support, or whatever else you can give? List at least three people.

What would it take for you to stop whatever you're doing and in some small way help one of those people in the next hour—rather than walking past the problem?

You see all kinds of needs every day. Is there anyone you shouldn't help? Explain your response.

Try answering these questions for some deep, long-term soul-searching: *What good deeds would you rather not do? What kinds of people are you most inclined to pass up? What places would you rather not go?*

RANDOM ACT NOTE

"Wherever there is a human being,
there is an opportunity for kindness."
—Seneca (4 BC–AD 65), Roman philosopher

WATCH/LISTEN/ASK

A need I noticed....

DO

How I acted to meet the need...

REPEAT

How my deed turned out—and how I might do it differently next time...

YOUR LIFE • GIVE AN ELDERLY NEIGHBOR A RIDE • SPONSOR A NEEDY CHILD • VOLUNTEER AT A

CHAPTER 19

WATCH AND DO

"I swore never to be silent whenever human beings endure suffering and humiliation. We must always take sides. Neutrality helps the oppressor, never the victim. Silence encourages the tormentor, never the tormented."

—Elie Wiesel (1928-), Holocaust survivor and author

"Determine a plan of action in the morning, and then evaluate yourself at night. How have you behaved today? What were your words, your deeds, your thoughts?"

—Thomas à Kempis (1380–1471), Christian monk

You might believe you're God's masterpiece, created to do good works. You might have caught a fever for passing along to others the same kindness God has shown you. You might be prepared to stand alone and keep doing good, even when it gets difficult. But what exactly are you supposed to do?

Often you can plan ahead—and like Thomas à Kempis suggests, check back with yourself to make sure you got the deed done. But other times you'll simply stumble on opportunities you could never have foreseen. Either way you'll find limitless openings if you consciously, intentionally, and thoughtfully begin to notice needs.

Start by looking around. **Watch!** What needs do you see? Of all the people you bump into each day, who most needs your help? What simple acts can you do to make a difference?

You can learn a lot with your eyes, but you figure out the details with your ears. **Listen!** What hurts do you hear expressed? How do people describe their needs in their own words? What do you learn by what they *don't* say?

When in doubt about what you can do to lend a hand, get more information. **Ask!** Don't assume you know everything. Don't barge into someone's space unless you're certain that your kind act will be welcome. In fact, it's always best to ask how you can help—if at all.

You know the next step. **Do!** Act on your concern. Do something with the information you gather. Make a real difference.

Once you've done all that, never stop. **Repeat!** Keep on believing that God made you to change the world, even when it seems crazy to do so. Even when you stand alone. Even when doing good gets difficult.

God made you to change the world every chance you get.

The apostle Paul writes, "Whenever we have the opportunity, we should do good to everyone..." (Galatians 6:10). So think back to your last few days—school, home, sports, clubs, music, whatever you did. Did you seize any chances to do good? What did you do?

What random acts of kindness did you miss? What can you still do to help?

Watch/Listen/Ask/Do/Repeat isn't rocket science. If that memory device doesn't strike you as helpful, how do you plan to actively notice the needs around you?

RANDOM ACT NOTE

"Wherever there is a human being,
there is an opportunity for kindness."
—Seneca (4 BC–AD 65), Roman philosopher

WATCH/LISTEN/ASK

A need I noticed....

DO

How I acted to meet the need...

REPEAT

How my deed turned out—and how I might do it differently next time...

CHAPTER 20

GET PRACTICAL

"Knowing is not enough; we must apply.
Willing is not enough; we must do."
—Johann Wolfgang von Goethe (1749-1832), German poet

"God is always calling on us to do the impossible. It helps me to remember that anything Jesus did during his life here on earth is something we should be able to do, too."
—Madeleine L'Engle (1918-), fantasy author

Those words from children's novelist Madeleine L'Engle may sound crazy—until you realize they reflect exactly what Jesus promises.

He tells his disciples, "I tell you the truth, anyone who believes in me will do the same works I have done, and even greater works, because I am going to be with the Father" (John 14:12 NLT). He implies in his next breath that the secret to these "greater works" is prayer (14:13-14).

Jesus couldn't have raised the bar any higher on what we can expect God to accomplish through us. But even as we dream high and wide, we have to land on some real-world actions.

As you try to act for good, enlist your friends. It's a law of life that any two brains in any room are smarter than yours alone, so here's an activity to try in whatever way that feels cool and not canned: Brainstorm with a few friends how you can change the world. Start with what you could do if you had a million dollars to fund your work, because that make-believe task can help you identify concerns you all really care about. Whittle down your thinking to what you can do with the cash you truly have at your disposal. Think of what sweat-effort deeds you can do without a penny in your pocket. And what can you do together that you can't do alone?

Still need a really easy and highly personal way to come up with ideas to do good? Scan the bottom of each page in this book. Circle the tasks that you can do especially well. Then go and do them.

If you could do one amazing deed to fix something wrong in the world, what would it be? Imagine you've got billions and billions of dollars to spend.

NEIGHBOR YOU DON'T KNOW WELL • COLLECT CANNED GOODS AND NON-PERISHABLES FOR YOUR

What's the best world-changing idea you can come up with—the kind where your gifts and passions intersect with needs you observe around you?

What five random acts from the bottom of the pages of this book best fit you? Write them underneath this question and attach a name to each. Also jot down a time or date you expect to get the deed done.

LOCAL SOUP KITCHEN OR FOOD BANK • GET TO KNOW SOMEONE OF ANOTHER RACE • BAKE

RANDOM ACT NOTE

"Wherever there is a human being,
there is an opportunity for kindness."
—Seneca (4 BC–AD 65), Roman philosopher

WATCH/LISTEN/ASK

A need I noticed....

DO

How I acted to meet the need...

REPEAT

How my deed turned out—and how I might do it differently next time...

FRESH BREAD FOR YOUR PRINCIPAL • BUY A WATER BUFFALO, GOAT, LLAMA, OR BABY CHICKS AT

CHAPTER 21

KEEP IT UP

"True happiness comes from the joy of deeds well done, the zest of creating things new."
—Antoine de Saint-Exupery (1900-1944), French author and aviator

"If you have love, you don't need to have anything else, and if you don't have it, it doesn't matter much what else you have."
—Sir James M. Barrie (1860-1937), Scottish novelist

You surely recognize the sucking sound emanating from some people who want your help. Somewhere in the midst of all your acting for good you'll likely feel worn out, used up, abused, maybe even doubtful of everything you're trying to accomplish. Sometimes you'll even get severely slammed for doing right. As playwright Clare Boothe Luce (1903-1987) once wryly noted: "No good deed goes unpunished."

Therefore when you help others, it's wise to learn to set boundaries and put your energies where they can make the most impact. But whatever your situation, God has an answer for your weariness. Through the apostle Paul he says, "Let us not become weary in doing good, for at the proper time we will reap a harvest if we do not give up" (Galatians 6:9).

If you get all of your food from the fridge or across a fast-food counter, it's easy to forget that green things take time to grow—as in four months, perhaps, between planting and harvest. Sometimes results from an act of kindness come sooner, but they might take even longer. So God says, "Don't get weary" and "Don't give up."

Why not? Because if you put the seed in the ground, the harvest will come. God says so. There's nothing more you can do—except maybe weed and water an ongoing need—because God himself ultimately is the one who makes things happen. And even if the situation you're trying to help never changes much, God will still produce a harvest within you. You'll be a different person because of what you've done.

What harvest are you expecting when you commit an act of kindness?

When have you felt most whipped from doing good? How did you keep at it—or not?

Agree or disagree with the following statement—and explain your response: *When you deal with needy people, it's better to err on the side of giving rather than the side of stinginess.*

God wants his care for you to power your care for others. Like Paul tells some early followers: "May our Lord Jesus Christ himself and God our Father, who loved us and by his grace gave us eternal encouragement and good hope, encourage your hearts and strengthen you in every good deed and word" (2 Thessalonians 2:16-17 TNIV). Take time right now to ask God to make you strong "in every good deed and word." Write your prayer here if you want.

A WEB SITE FOR SERVICE AGENCIES IN YOUR COMMUNITY TO ADVERTISE THEIR NEEDS AND

RANDOM ACT NOTE

"Wherever there is a human being,
there is an opportunity for kindness."
—Seneca (4 BC–AD 65), Roman philosopher

WATCH/LISTEN/ASK

A need I noticed....

DO

How I acted to meet the need...

REPEAT

How my deed turned out—and how I might do it differently next time...

CHAPTER 22

BE STEALTHY

"Noble deeds that are concealed are most esteemed."
—Blaise Pascal (1623–1662),
French mathematician and religious philosopher

"Big words seldom accompany good deeds."
—Charlotte Whitton (1896-1975),
mayor of Ottawa, Canada's national capitol

So you've decided you want to be God's agent for good. But there's one thing you surely don't aspire to be: a "goody two-shoes."

You might assume that slam originated with your parents' generation as a playground smack for peers who tattled to the local authority figures. But the term has actually been around for nearly 250 years. "The History of Goody Two-Shoes" was an English story about a girl, Goody, who owned just a single shoe. When she received a pair of shoes she was so pleased that she showed them off to everyone, boasting "two shoes, two shoes." So now the phrase refers to a pompous, smug, self-righteous person.

Jesus warns against deliberately parading our good acts for everyone else to see: "Be especially careful when you are trying to be good so that you don't make a performance out of it. It might be good theater, but the God who made you won't be applauding. When you do something for someone else, don't call attention to yourself" (Matthew 6:1-2 MSG). "When you give to someone in need," he adds, "don't let your left hand know what your right hand is doing. Give your gifts in private, and your Father, who sees everything, will reward you" (6:3-4 NLT).

Many good deeds can't help being noticed, but that's different from smearing your goodness in others' faces. When you do kind acts, your aim isn't to play to the crowds. It's to please an audience of one—God above all.

Not to be mean, but when have you seen people do good just to get noticed?

When you do good and do it well, how do you guard against coming off as the dreaded Goody Two-Shoes?

Like Philippians 2:13 says, our inclinations and abilities come from God: "It is God who works in you to will and to act in order to fulfill his good purpose." So how can you give credit to God without sounding or acting hyper-spiritual?

TRUTH: Recall an instance when you put down a sibling for not knowing how to do something.

DARE: Find a way to help that sibling this week.

BOOKS, VIDEOS, OR DVDS YOU'VE OUTGROWN TO A WORTHY RECIPIENT • TAKE A PARKING SPOT AT

RANDOM ACT NOTE

"Wherever there is a human being,
there is an opportunity for kindness."
—Seneca (4 BC–AD 65), Roman philosopher

WATCH/LISTEN/ASK

A need I noticed....

DO

How I acted to meet the need...

REPEAT

How my deed turned out—and how I might do it differently next time...

THE FAR END OF THE LOT • MAKE A DEAL WITH A GAS STATION IN A NEEDY PART OF TOWN—PAY

CHAPTER 23

SPOT JESUS

"We can do little things for God: I turn the cake that is frying on the pan, for love of him; and that done, if there is nothing else to call me, I prostrate myself in worship before him who has given me grace to work; afterwards I rise happier than a king."

—Brother Lawrence (1605–1691), Christian monk

"Each one of them is Jesus in disguise."

—Mother Teresa (1910-1997), founder of the Missionaries of Charity in Calcutta, India

---

According to Jesus, people who do good are in for a surprise at the end of time.

Here's how it will go down, with a mob of God-followers gathered around his throne: "Then the King will say to those on his right, 'Come, you who are blessed by my Father; take your inheritance, the kingdom prepared for you since the creation of the world. For I was hungry and you gave me something to eat, I was thirsty and you gave me something to drink, I was a stranger and you invited me in, I needed clothes and you clothed me, I was sick and you looked after me, I was in prison and you came to visit me'" (Matthew 25:34-36).

"But when?" they will say. "When did we do those things—feed you... or give you a drink...or invite you in...or clothe you, comfort you, or visit you?"

Jesus will answer, "When you did it to one of the least of these my brothers and sisters, you were doing it to me!" (Matthew 25:40).

Whether you know it or not, you meet Jesus every time you help someone in need. Most people who benefit from your kindness won't look anything like Jesus, though. They might have creaky bones, snotty noses, grouchy attitudes, ungrateful words.

But the most important thing to remember is, when you serve them, you serve Jesus.

Do you find that your experiences of doing good scream, "I'm face-to-face with Jesus!" Why—or why not?

SOMEONE YOU'RE THINKING OF HER AND PRAYING FOR HER—AS LONG AS YOU ACTUALLY ARE •

Is it true that you're serving Jesus every time you do good? Why does it matter?

Some Christians believe the only place to meet Jesus is in daily devotions or a well-choreographed worship service. Other people swear they've never once spotted Jesus inside the walls of any church building. Check out this quote from Augustine of Hippo (354–430) and explain what it has to do with how you experience closeness to God: "No man has a right to lead such a life of contemplation as to forget in his own ease the service due to his neighbor; nor has any man a right to be so immersed in active life as to neglect the contemplation of God."

RANDOM ACT NOTE

"Wherever there is a human being,
there is an opportunity for kindness."
—Seneca (4 BC–AD 65), Roman philosopher

WATCH/LISTEN/ASK

A need I noticed....

DO

How I acted to meet the need...

REPEAT

How my deed turned out—and how I might do it differently next time...

FOR BUILD-YOUR-OWN SUNDAES • FEED EXPIRED PARKING METERS (OR ALMOST-EXPIRED METERS)

CHAPTER 24

LIVE ON

"Imagination is everything. It is the preview of life's coming attractions."
—Albert Einstein (1879-1955), physicist

"I expect to pass through this world but once; any good thing, therefore, that I can do, or any kindness that I can show to my fellow creatures, let me do it now; let me not defer or neglect it, for I shall not pass this way again."
—Marcus Aurelius (121–180), the last of the "Five Good Emperors" of Rome

---

When the human race took a diving leap into sin, God wasn't content to leave us in our broken state. He's not even happy with the same-old, same-old. He wants us to be in even better condition than at the start, even if it takes all eternity to accomplish that. So even though we rejected him, he decided to give us mercy so we could spread mercy. As the simple saying goes, "We love because he first loved us" (1 John 4:19).

Your enthusiasm to be part of his plan to change the world can easily fizzle. His commands can sound crazy.

Acting for good can mean you stand alone. And doing right can get difficult. If you want to continue to develop a rhythm of life where you share with others the same care God showers on you, then you'll want to consciously give yourself to God each day.

English poet and hymnwriter Frances Ridley Havergal (1836–1879) tells how to hand your life over to God for his amazing purposes. Chew on this quote and figure out a way to tell God each day—in your own words—that you want to live for him: "Begin at once; before you venture away from this quiet moment, ask your King to take you wholly into his service, and place all the hours of this day quite simply at his disposal, and ask him to make and keep you ready to do just exactly what he appoints. Never mind about tomorrow; one day at a time is enough. Try it today, and see if it is not a day of strange, almost curious peace, so sweet that you will be only too thankful when tomorrow comes to ask him to take it also."

How do you attempt to better understand and experience God's love for you so you can keep on loving others?

LAUNDROMAT AND PAY FOR EVERYONE'S WASHING AND DRYING CYCLES • VOLUNTEER AT A

Why would you want to live each day for God's good purposes—or not?

What do you think God has planned for your future as you live for him?

How will your world be different if you change the world every chance you get?

RANDOM ACT NOTE

"Wherever there is a human being,
there is an opportunity for kindness."
—*Seneca (4 BC–AD 65), Roman philosopher*

WATCH/LISTEN/ASK

A need I noticed....

DO

How I acted to meet the need...

REPEAT

How my deed turned out—and how I might do it differently next time...